Read All About
DINOSAURS

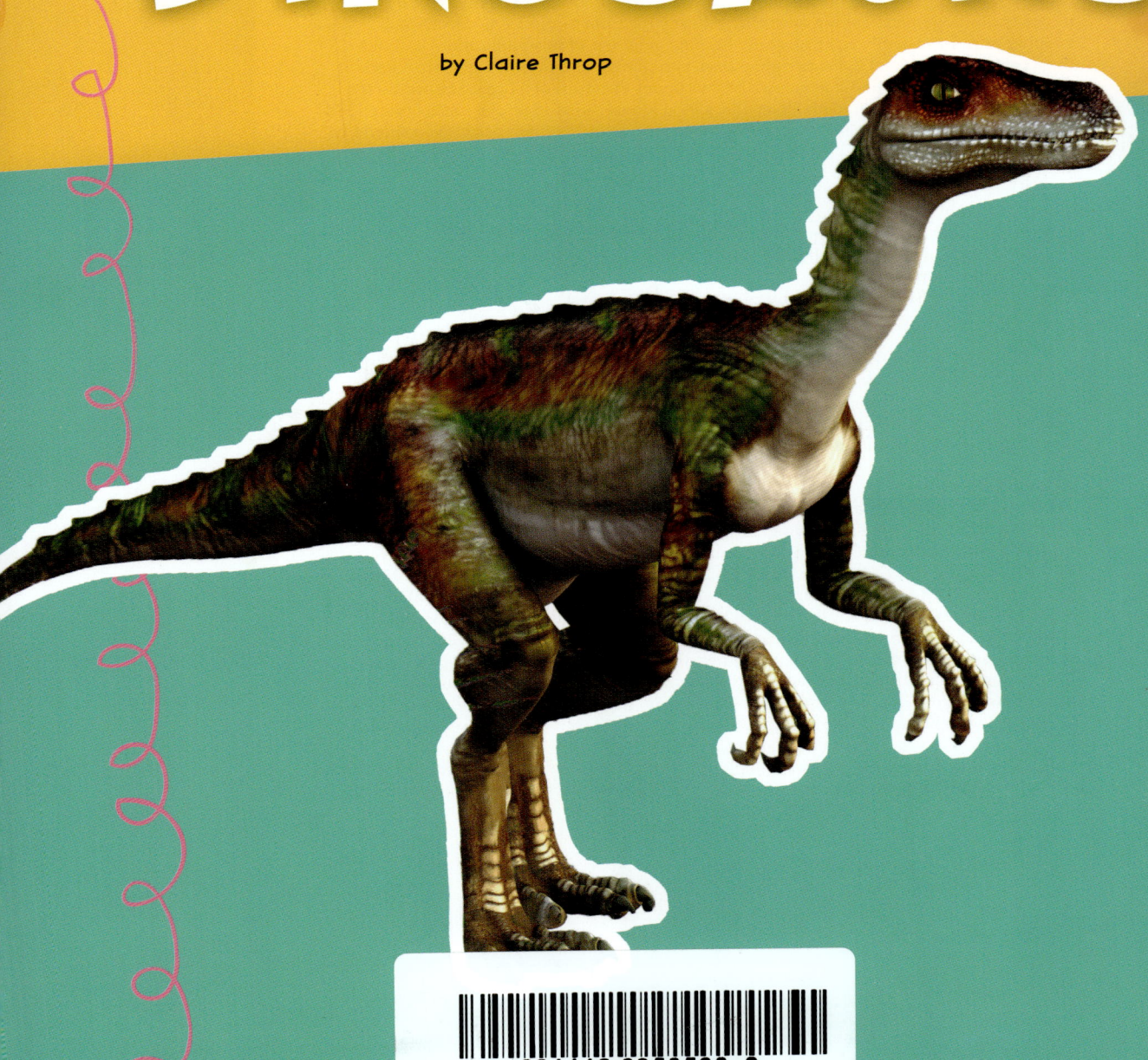

by Claire Throp

Raintree is an imprint of Capstone Global Library Limited, a company incorporated in England and Wales having its registered office at 264 Banbury Road, Oxford, OX2 7DY – Registered company number: 6695582

www.raintree.co.uk
myorders@raintree.co.uk

Hardback edition © Capstone Global Library Limited 2022
Paperback edition © Capstone Global Library Limited 2023
The moral rights of the proprietor have been asserted.

All rights reserved. No part of this publication may be reproduced in any form or by any means (including photocopying or storing it in any medium by electronic means and whether or not transiently or incidentally to some other use of this publication) without the written permission of the copyright owner, except in accordance with the provisions of the Copyright, Designs and Patents Act 1988 or under the terms of a licence issued by the Copyright Licensing Agency, 5th Floor, Shackleton House, 4 Battle Bridge Lane, London SE1 2HX (www.cla.co.uk). Applications for the copyright owner's written permission should be addressed to the publisher.

Edited by Peter Mavrikis
Designed by Kayla Rossow
Original illustrations © Capstone Global Library Limited 2022
Picture research by Morgan Walters
Production by Laura Manthe
Originated by Capstone Global Library Ltd
Printed and bound in India

978 1 3982 2582 4 (hardback)
978 1 3982 2581 7 (paperback)

British Library Cataloguing in Publication Data
A full catalogue record for this book is available from the British Library.

Acknowledgements
We would like to thank the following for permission to reproduce photographs: Alamy: MERVYN REES, bottom 31Bottom of Form, Nature Picture Library, bottom 30, The Natural History Museum, top 30; iStockphoto: 49pauly, top 26; Jon Hughes, top right Cover, bottom Cover, 1, 4, 5, 7, 8, 9, 10, 11, 12, 13, 14, 15, 17, 18, 19, 20, top 21, 22, top 23, 24, 25, 28; Newscom: Darryl Bush/ZUMApress, 16, Gerard LACZ/NHPA/Photoshot, top 31, Hannibal Hanschke/REUTERS, top 14; Science Source: Millard H. Sharp, bottom 29; Shutterstock: Anatoliy Lukich, top 25, Herschel Hoffmeyer, bottom 12, bottom 21, hjochen, bottom 26, Jemastock, design element throughout, KanokpolTokumhnerd, (watercolor) Cover, Kelvin Degree, design element throughout, Kostyantyn Ivanyshen, bottom 23, Lefteris Papaulakis, top 28, Marcio Jose Bastos Silva, bottom 6, MikhailSh, top 27, Rafael Trafaniuc, top 6, ReVelStockArt, design element throughout, sarkao, top 29, sdecoret, bottom left 7, xrender, bottom 27

Every effort has been made to contact copyright holders of material reproduced in this book. Any omissions will be rectified in subsequent printings if notice is given to the publisher.

Contents

Chapter 1
When did dinosaurs live?..........4

Chapter 2
Meat eaters..................8

Chapter 3
Plant eaters.................16

Chapter 4
In the air...................24

Chapter 5
In the sea..................28

Glossary 32
Index 32

Words in **bold** are in the glossary.

Chapter 1

When did dinosaurs live?

Dinosaurs lived many millions of years ago, in **prehistoric** times.

Dinosaurs were around for more than 160 million years! The time that dinosaurs lived is broken into three periods.

The Triassic Period was 252 to 201 million years ago. Eoraptors lived at this time.

The Jurassic Period was 201 to 145 million years ago. Allosaurus lived during this time.

The Cretaceous Period was 145 to 66 million years ago. Edmontosaurus lived at this time.

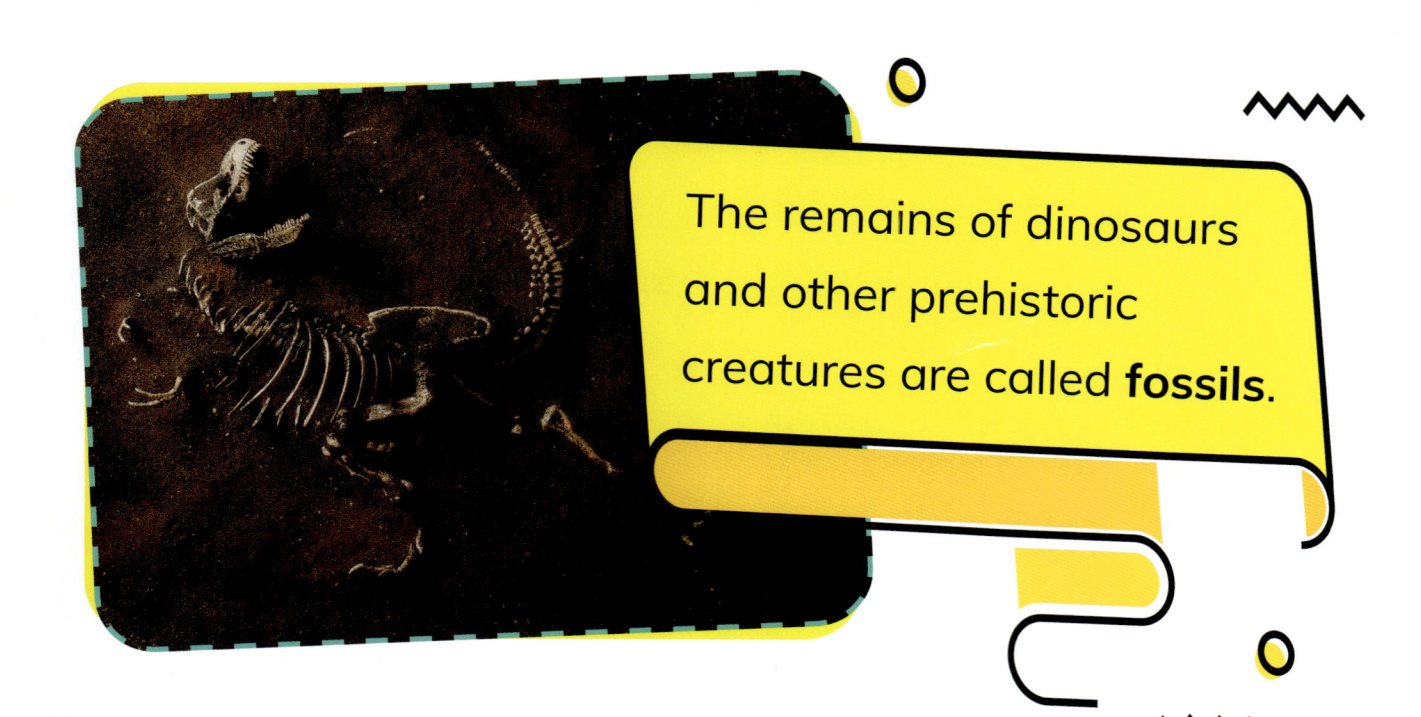

The remains of dinosaurs and other prehistoric creatures are called **fossils**.

People from China found the first dinosaur fossils more than 2,000 years ago. They thought the bones were from giant dragons!

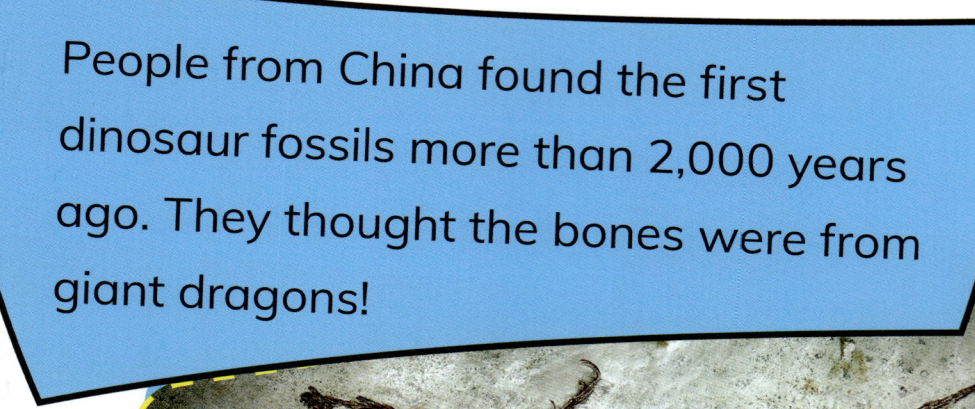

The word dinosaur comes from deinos, which means "terrible", and sauros, which means "lizard".

There were more than 700 **species** of dinosaurs!

About 66 million years ago, a huge rock from space hit Earth. It caused the dinosaurs to die out.

Chapter 2

Meat eaters

Some dinosaurs ate other dinosaurs! They usually had strong legs, large jaws, sharp teeth and claws.

Herrerasaurus was one of the earliest dinosaurs. It had teeth that curved inwards to help it hold on to **prey**.

Eoraptor had three toes at the front of each foot and one at the back.

Many meat-eating dinosaurs were theropods. They walked on their back legs.

Allosaurus probably ate the remains of dead animals as well as being a hunter.

Megalosaurus was the first dinosaur to be named. Megalosaurus means "great lizard".

The largest dinosaur tooth ever found belonged to a Tyrannosaurus rex. The tooth was 30 centimetres (12 inches) long!

Most dinosaurs are now thought to have had feathers. Even the scary Tyrannosaurus rex – or "lizard king" – may have had feathers!

Saltopus was the size of a cat. Its name means "hopping foot".

One of the fastest dinosaurs was Dromiceiomimus. It could run at more than 64 kilometres (40 miles) per hour!

Struthiomimus means "ostrich **mimic**". It looked like an ostrich!

Coelophysis was a small theropod. It probably hunted in groups.

Cryolophosaurus was originally called Elvisaurus! This is because the crest on its head looked like Elvis Presley's hairstyle!

Spinosaurus was the first dinosaur that could swim. It had a nose high on its head like a crocodile. It also had paddle-like feet like a duck.

Troodon had a large brain compared to the size of its body.

Utahraptor was heavier than a grizzly bear!

Baryonyx had a claw that grew to about 30 centimetres (1 foot). It used its claw to hook fish to eat.

Chapter 3

Plant eaters

Some dinosaurs ate only plants. These included sauropods, ankylosaurs and euornithopods.

Plant eaters were bigger than meat eaters. Scientists guess how big a dinosaur was by measuring its thigh bone.

thigh bone

Sauropods such as Brachiosaurus had very long necks and tiny heads.

Cetiosaurus was huge – about 18 m (59 feet) in length! Its name means "whale lizard".

Ankylosaurs had **armour** to protect their short, heavy bodies. It was made up of bony plates and spikes.

Stegosaurus could be 8 m (27 feet) long. But its brain was about the size of a walnut!

An ankylosaur called Euoplocephalus even had armoured eyelids!

Hadrosaurs are sometimes called duck-billed dinosaurs because of the shape of their snouts.

Some plant-eating dinosaurs such as the Stegoceras walked on two legs. Stegoceras means "horny roof".

Mary Ann Mantell found the first iguanodon tooth in England in 1822.

Plant-eating dinosaurs probably farted a lot! Plants are hard to break down. A gas called methane is the result.

Ceratopsians had beaks, frills around their necks and sometimes horns. They lived 145 to 66 million years ago.

Triceratops' frill could measure 1 m (3 feet) across!

The Psittacosaurus had a beak. Psittacus is the Latin word for parrot.

Some dinosaurs such as Gallimimus ate both plants and meat.

Chapter 4

In the air

Some prehistoric creatures spent time in the air. Some flew like birds. Others just glided.

Pterosaur means "wing lizard".

raven

Pterosaurs were the first flying **reptiles**. Did you know that the birds outside your window are related to the dinosaurs?

In 2020, fossils of three new species of toothed pterosaurs were found in Morocco. Their wings were nearly 4 m (13 feet) wide!

Like birds today, dinosaurs laid eggs. Some were coloured and patterned.

A tiny, bird-like fossil has been found in **amber**. It is at least 99 million years old. It is the smallest known dinosaur.

Archaeopteryx weighed only about 500 grams (1 pound).

Tiny creatures called lice have been found on some feathered dinosaur fossils.

Chapter 5

In the sea

Some prehistoric creatures lived in the sea. These included plesiosaurs, ichthyosaurs and ammonites.

plesiosaur

Liopleurodons could smell their prey even underwater.

Ammonites had sharp, beak-like jaws and long arms that reached out from their shells to grab prey.

Xiphactinus could swallow its prey whole – even fish that measured 2 m (6 feet) long!

Coprolites are fossils of dinosaur poo. Spiral-shaped poos up to 30 cm (1 foot) long were probably left by **ancient** sharks.

Frilled sharks have been around for 80 million years. They have about 300 teeth!

Glossary

amber yellowish-brown substance made from fossilized tree sap

ancient from a very long time ago

armour bones, scales and skin that some animals have on their bodies to protect them

fossil remains of an ancient plant or animal that have hardened into rock

mimic copy

prehistoric time before history was written down

prey animal hunted by another animal for food

reptile cold-blooded animal that breathes air and has a backbone

species group of animals with similar features

Index

bones 16, 18
Cretaceous Period 5
eating 8, 9, 15, 16, 20, 21, 23, 29
feathers 11, 27
flying 24, 25
fossils 6, 26, 27, 30
Jurassic Period 5
prey 8, 28, 29
reptiles 25
species 7
swimming 14
teeth 10, 20, 25
theropods 9, 13
Triassic Period 4

A jawbone found in England belonged to an ichthyosaur that was nearly 26 m (85 feet) in length. That's almost as big as a blue whale!

The coelacanth was thought to have died out with the dinosaurs. But it was rediscovered in 1938!